FEMA Benefit-Cost Analysis Re-engineering (BCAR)

Damage-Frequency Assessment (DFA)

(Limited Data Module/Unknown Frequency Determination)

Methodology Report

Version 4.5

May 2009

Contents

Tables

Figures

Purpose

This BCAR report is provided for use by interested BCA users to review and understand the methodology behind the FEMA Damage Frequency Assessment (DFA) Module – previously known as the FEMA Limited Data Module for Benefit-Cost Analysis (LD Module) - and determining unknown frequencies within the LD Module. The methodology report was reviewed by the FEMA BCAR Technical Advisory Group (TAG), and is part of a larger effort to re-engineer the FEMA Benefit-Cost Analysis (BCA) methods, modules, guidance, and training in order to improve the BCA process.

Overview of Problem Statements

The URS BCAR Team and the FEMA BCAR TAG identified the following problem statements as issues that needed to be addressed in the LD Module:

1. Determine Unknown Frequencies (BCAR Issue No. LD-003)

2. Update the FEMA Inflation Calculator and Include in the LD Module (BCAR Issue No. LD-001)

3. Improve Guidance on Use of the LD Module (BCAR Issue No. LD-002)

4. Improve Guidance on After-Mitigation Damages for the LD Module (BCAR Issue No. LD-002)

Each of these problem statements and the methodologies adopted to address them are described in greater detail in the sections that follow.

Problem Statement 1: Determine Unknown Frequencies

The FEMA Limited Data Module for benefit-cost analysis (LD Module) was developed to calculate project benefits and costs for proposed hazard mitigation projects based on two or more historic damage events. The main advantage of the LD Module is its flexibility: it can be used for a wide range of hazards and mitigation project facilities. Unlike FEMA's Full Data Modules for flood, wind and earthquake, the LD Module does not require specific hazard and building site data. However, the primary disadvantage with the LD Module is that the frequencies of the historic hazard events must be determined in order to compute the project benefits. Determining frequencies of historic hazard events is problematic because most hazards do not have standard recurrence intervals that can be used to establish frequencies of historic events; while other hazards, such as floods, that do have standard recurrence intervals cannot be used to establish frequencies of historic events because the data is incomplete, inaccurate, or out of date. As a result, many applicants do not consistently or accurately determine the frequencies of historic hazard events, which yield incorrect benefit-cost ratios.

In order to address this problem, an alternate estimation technique was developed to estimate frequencies for unknown event frequencies. The technique was outlined in Section 1.5.3 of the Flood Data Derivation document on the FEMA Mitigation BCA Toolkit CD (Version 3.0, July 2006), and could be used for any hazard, provided the following conditions were met:

1. There is a minimum of three hazard events,

2. There is a period of at least 5 years,

3. It is a localized flood/hazard event (i.e., flood depths are within 0.5 feet on average among buildings/facilities), and

4. No other method is available to tie historic events to frequencies.

Once these conditions were met, the alternate estimation technique required that all historic event damages be updated to the present value using the FEMA Inflation Calculator on the FEMA Mitigation BCA Toolkit CD. The next step was to group the historic event damages into groups based on the total damage repair cost. Although the BCA Toolkit CD did not provide definitive guidance or mathematical formulas on how to divide the historic event damages into groups other than by visual comparison of the damage values, the technique can be illustrated using the following example.

A residential building constructed in 1964 had documentation for flood claims that started in 1966. The building experienced six floods in a 40-year period of known data from 1966 to 2006, as shown on the next page.

Event Year	Current Value of Damage
1966	$2,500
1970	$20,000
1971	$3,200
1980	$4,500
1988	$5,600
2005	$23,000
Total	**$53,000**

Based on the data above, floods occur approximately every 7 years on average (6 events in 40 years). The 1970 and 2005 events are more significant floods than the others as reflected by the value of damage, and are, by definition, less probable events. For this reason, the damages from the 1970 and 2005 events cannot be merged with those from the other floods. However, the damages from those less significant floods 1966 and 1971 can reasonably be merged and averaged. Similarly, the damages from 1980 and 1988 can reasonably be merged and averaged. Based on these groupings, the two smallest events (1966 and 1971) have an average return period of 7 years (6 events of the same value or greater in 40 years) with an average damage value of $2,850. Next, the two mid-range events (1980 and 1988) have an average return period of 10 years (4 events of the same value or greater in 40 years) and an average value of $5,050. Finally, the two largest events (1970 and 2005) have a return period of 20 years (2 events of the same value and none greater in 40 years) and an average damage value of $21,500. Refer to the summary tables below for these calculations.

Group 1

Item	Value
Events	6
Period	40 years (1966 to 2006)
Average Return Period	7 years (40 years / 6 events)
Average Damages per Event	$2,850 ([$2,500 + $3,200]/2)

Group 2

Item	Value
Events	4
Period	40 years (1966 to 2006)
Average Return Period	10 years (40 years / 4 events)
Average Damages per Event	$5,050 ([$4,500 + $5,600]/2)

Group 3

Item	Value
Events	2
Period	40 years (1966 to 2006)
Average Return Period	20 years (40 years / 2 events)
Average Damages per Event	$21,500 ([$20,000 + $23,000]/2)

Although the establishment of the alternate estimation technique addressed some of the difficulties associated with determining unknown frequencies, problems with BCA results continued because many applicants did not understand or correctly apply the alternate estimation technique. Based on feedback from BCA applicants and users, there was an urgent need to develop and automate a standard methodology to consistently estimate the frequencies of unknown historic events for use in the LD Module.

Alternative Methodologies to Address Problem Statement 1

The following alternate methodologies were proposed to address the problem of unknown frequency determinations:

1. Standardize and automate the alternate estimation technique to determine unknown frequencies

2. Establish a revised statistical analysis technique to determine unknown frequencies

Each of these alternate methodologies are described in the sections that follow.

Methodology 1: Standardize and Automate the Alternate Estimation Technique

This first methodology applies the alternate estimation technique from Section 1.5.3 of the Flood Data Derivation document on the FEMA Mitigation BCA Toolkit CD (Version 3.0, July 2006) to establish a standardized and automated process for determining unknown frequencies. At this stage, the automated process has been converted into a spreadsheet tool that consists of the following steps:

Step 1 - Input Historic Damage and Indicate Basis for Frequencies: In step 1, the user inputs the dollar damages, losses, and dates associated with historic damage events. In addition, the user indicates if the frequencies of historic damage events are known or unknown. If the frequencies of historic damage events are known, the user inputs the frequency of each event in years and selects the basis for the frequency determinations. In addition, documentation must be provided to support the known frequency determinations. Once this is done, the spreadsheet tool automatically updates all historic damages input by the user to the current year of analysis using the FEMA Inflation Calculator, and the user proceeds to Step 2 or Step 3.

Step 2 – Sort Damages and Estimate Inputs for Known Frequency Events: If the user inputs known frequencies for all historic damage events in Step 1, the user may then use a program macro to sort inflated damage values using the existing FEMA Inflation Calculator based on known frequencies, as illustrated in Figure 1. Once this is done, the program automatically groups events by frequency and computes the average damages and losses for each frequency, as illustrated in Figure 2. The information in Figure 2 is then input into the LD Module to estimate the project damages before mitigation, which can be used to determine the project benefits.

VALUES SORTED BY KNOWN EVENT FREQUNECIES					
Frequency (years)	Damage Estimate (Current Dollars)			Loss of Function Time (days)	Total Damage Estimate (Current $)
	A	B	C		
5	$1,620	$4,049	$1,620	1	$11,317
5	$2,060	$5,150	$2,060	1	$13,299
10	$3,143	$7,858	$3,143	2	$22,201
10	$4,371	$7,649	$4,371	2	$24,448
10	$4,164	$8,327	$4,164	2	$24,712
10	$3,850	$9,626	$3,850	2	$25,384
15	$4,434	$9,501	$4,434	2	$26,426
15	$4,467	$11,168	$4,467	2	$28,160
15	$4,655	$11,637	$4,655	2	$29,005
15	$5,314	$13,285	$5,314	2	$31,970
25	$10,729	$26,823	$10,729	3	$60,368
25	$11,026	$27,565	$11,026	3	$61,703
25	$15,074	$22,611	$15,074	3	$64,845
50	$17,456	$43,640	$17,456	3	$90,638
50	$18,627	$46,567	$18,627	3	$95,907
70	$27,920	$69,800	$27,920	3	$137,726
75	$30,705	$76,762	$30,705	4	$154,287
80	$41,792	$59,703	$41,792	4	$159,401
80	$32,472	$81,181	$32,472	5	$166,270
100	$35,003	$87,507	$35,003	5	$177,656

Figure 1. Sorting of Inflated Damage Values Based on Known Event Frequencies

Hazard Frequency Events (years)	Scenario Damages			Loss of Function Time and Dollars		TOTAL Damages and Losses
	A	B	C	Days	Losses	
5	$1,840	$4,600	$1,840	1.00	$4,029	$12,308
10	$3,882	$8,365	$3,882	2.00	$8,058	$24,186
15	$4,717	$11,398	$4,717	2.00	$8,058	$28,890
25	$12,276	$25,666	$12,276	3.00	$12,086	$62,305
50	$18,041	$45,103	$18,041	3.00	$12,086	$93,272
70	$27,920	$69,800	$27,920	3.00	$12,086	$137,726
75	$30,705	$76,762	$30,705	4.00	$16,115	$154,287
80	$37,132	$70,442	$37,132	4.50	$18,129	$162,835
100	$35,003	$87,507	$35,003	5.00	$20,144	$177,656

Figure 2. Grouping Known Event Frequency Damages for Input into the LD Module

Step 3 –Sort Damages and Estimate Inputs for Unknown Frequency Events: If the user does not know the frequencies for all historic damage events in Step 1, the user may then use a program macro to sort inflated damage values in ascending order based on total damages, as illustrated in Figure 3. Once this is done, the program applies the alternate estimation technique using the following equations to group events and determine unknown frequencies:

Event 1:
$$E_1 = \left[\frac{\sum_{i=1}^{n} D_i}{n} \right] \qquad \text{for} \qquad D_i \leq 1.5 D_1$$

Frequency 1:
$$f_1 = \frac{AD}{t}$$

Event 2:
$$E_2 = \left[\frac{\sum_{j=n+1}^{p} D_j}{(p-n)} \right] \qquad \text{for} \qquad D_j \leq 1.5 D_{n+1}$$

Frequency 2:
$$f_2 = \frac{AD}{(t-n)}$$

Event 3:
$$E_3 = \left[\frac{\sum\limits_{k=p+1}^{r} D_k}{(r-p)} \right]$$
for $D_k \leq 1.5 D_{p+1}$

Frequency 3: $f_3 = \dfrac{AD}{(t-p)}$ etc.

Where: AD = the analysis duration, also known as the period of record (in years)

D = a historic damage occurrence (in current dollars)

E = an event group consisting of one or more historic damage occurrences, expressed as an average historic damage occurrence (in current dollars)

f = the frequency associated with an event group (in years)

t = the total number of historic damage occurrences of magnitude E_1 or greater within the analysis duration/period of record

(t - n) = the total number of historic damage occurrences of magnitude E_2 or greater within the analysis duration/period of record

(t − p) = the total number of historic damage occurrences of magnitude E_3 or greater within the analysis duration/period of record

The current spreadsheet program applies these formulas as follows: the minimum initial occurrence 1 is associated with event group 1. If the value of occurrence 2 is less than 150 percent of the value of occurrence 1, then occurrence 2 is part of event group 1. However, if occurrence 2 equals or exceeds 150 percent of occurrence 1, then occurrence 2 becomes the minimum value for event group 2, and the cycle continues. Once all the occurrences are grouped into events, the program automatically computes the average damages and losses for each event group. Finally, the program uses the alternate estimation technique to determine the unknown event frequencies based on the total number of events that are greater than or equal to that event within the period of record input by the user, as illustrated in Figure 4. The information in Figure 4 is then input into the LD Module to estimate the project damages before mitigation, which can be used to determine the project benefits.

VALUES SORTED BY TOTAL DAMAGE				
Damage Estimate (Current Dollars)			Loss of Function	Total Damage
A	B	C	Time (days)	Estimate (Current $)
$931	$1,861	$931	0.5	$5,737
$982	$1,964	$982	0.5	$5,943
$2,060	$4,120	$2,060	1	$12,269
$2,185	$4,371	$2,185	1	$12,771
$4,478	$8,955	$4,478	2	$25,968
$4,750	$9,501	$4,750	2	$27,059
$4,857	$9,715	$4,857	2	$27,487
$10,729	$26,823	$10,729	3	$60,368
$11,026	$27,565	$11,026	3	$61,703
$15,074	$22,611	$15,074	3	$64,845
$24,354	$48,709	$24,354	4	$113,532
$26,184	$52,368	$26,184	4	$120,851
$51,337	$102,675	$51,337	5	$225,493
$58,338	$116,676	$58,338	5	$253,495
$85,022	$170,045	$85,022	7	$368,291
$93,099	$186,197	$93,099	7	$400,596
$144,995	$289,991	$144,995	10	$620,269
$158,213	$316,426	$158,213	10	$673,140
$242,958	$485,915	$242,958	14	$1,028,233
$242,958	$485,915	$242,958	14	$1,028,233

Figure 3. Sorting of Inflated Damage Values Based on Total Damage

Hazard Frequency Events (years)	Scenario Damages			Loss of Function Time and Dollars		TOTAL Damages and Losses
	A	B	C	Days	Losses	
10.3	$956	$1,913	$956	0.50	$2,014	$5,840
11.4	$2,123	$4,245	$2,123	1.00	$4,029	$12,520
12.8	$4,695	$9,390	$4,695	2.00	$8,058	$26,838
15.8	$12,276	$25,666	$12,276	3.00	$12,086	$62,305
20.5	$25,269	$50,538	$25,269	4.00	$16,115	$117,192
25.6	$54,838	$109,675	$54,838	5.00	$20,144	$239,494
34.2	$89,061	$178,121	$89,061	7.00	$28,201	$384,443
51.3	$151,604	$303,209	$151,604	10.00	$40,288	$151,604
102.5	$242,958	$485,915	$242,958	14.00	$56,403	$1,028,233

Figure 4. Grouping Unknown Event Frequency Damages for Input into the LD Module

This second methodology applies a technique based on statistical analysis principles to establish a revised automated process for determining unknown frequencies. A description of the calculation procedures and equations for this alternative methodology to obtain a Recurrence Interval (RI) of damages is provided on the pages that follow and summarized using the flow diagram at the end of this section. Note that this approach applies only to the inflated values of total annual damages. Therefore, if more than one damage event occurs in a given year, the user needs to add the damages together and use the sum of the damages for that given year in the input section.

The calculation procedure for this alternative methodology has been implemented in a revised spreadsheet tool that has been designed to run without invoking any macros, thus enhancing its interaction with the overall BCA interface under development as part of the BCAR initiative. Note that calculation assumptions and details of methods and equations are not provided here.

The spreadsheet has a simple input/output structure and all calculations are conducted in the background with no need for user interaction. Calculation parameters - such as criteria for grouping damages together or the uncertainty percentage in setting an upper limit of high outlier - that could otherwise have been a user-provided variable, are fixed to appropriate numbers by experiment. Therefore, all potential users of the tool will obtain the same RI damage result for the same data.

> **Data Input:** In the first input section, the user provides the year of analysis (typically the current year) and the year the structure was built in order to compute the age of the structure or Structure Life (SL). The User-Input Analysis Duration (UIAD) also needs to be input if the period of available data record is shorter than the age of the structure. If the user provides a value for Analysis Duration (AD), then the spreadsheet tool uses this value (AD = UIAD); otherwise, the analysis duration is set to the age of the structure (AD = SL). Note that in the latest version of the software, the guidance for determining the Period of Record is further developed - refer to Problem Statement 3 for additional details. In the next input section, the user must provide the damage year and the corresponding total damage dollar values with unknown recurrence interval (DVURI) for each event. If there is more than one damage event in a given year, the sum of all damage values for that year must be input as one damage value. The user may also input one or two historical damage values with known recurrence interval(s) (DVKRI) provided that the known RI(s) is larger than the period of analysis and is documented from credible sources. If these conditions are not met, then the user can simply input these events as events with unknown

recurrence interval (DVURIs). Figure 5 shows an example of the input section of the spreadsheet with numbers input from a sample problem.

INPUT						
Analysis Year (4 digit year)	Year Built (4 digit year)	Analysis Duration (years)	User Input Analysis Duartion (years)			
2007	1970	38				
Historical Damage Data						
Damages with Unknown Recurrence Interval			Damages with Known Recurrence Interval			
Damage Year (4 digit year)	Total damage (dollars)	Damages inflated to analysis Year (dollars)	Damage Year (4 digit year)	Total damage (dollars)	Known Recurrence Interval (years)	Damages inflated to analysis Year (dollars)
1974	$9,000	$38,626	1971	$12,200	100	$63,724
1989	$8,000	$13,647	1980	$16,200	50	$41,583
1991	$12,000	$18,630	User Notes:			
1997	$10,000	$13,174				
2000	$7,000	$8,609				
2001	$4,500	$5,373				

Figure 5. The Input Section of the Tool with Numbers from a Sample Analysis

Damage Value Inflation, Data Sorting and Visual Comparison to Log-Normal Distribution: Once the data is input, the spreadsheet tool then inflates all damage values to the year of analysis, sorts the inflated damages, and calculates a preliminary RI for each event considering only the years with damages. In the original version of the spreadsheet, the inflation calculations are done consistent with the current FEMA Inflation Calculator. This is shown in Figure 5. Note that the latest version of the spreadsheet tool has been updated to utilize the latest version of the FEMA Inflation Calculator developed by the URS BCAR Team – refer to Problem Statement 2 for additional details.

A log-normal distribution is fit to the processed damage data and then adjusted for total probability. The results are shown on a graph for visual comparison with spreadsheet results. Figure 6 shows an example of this graph with numbers from a sample analysis.

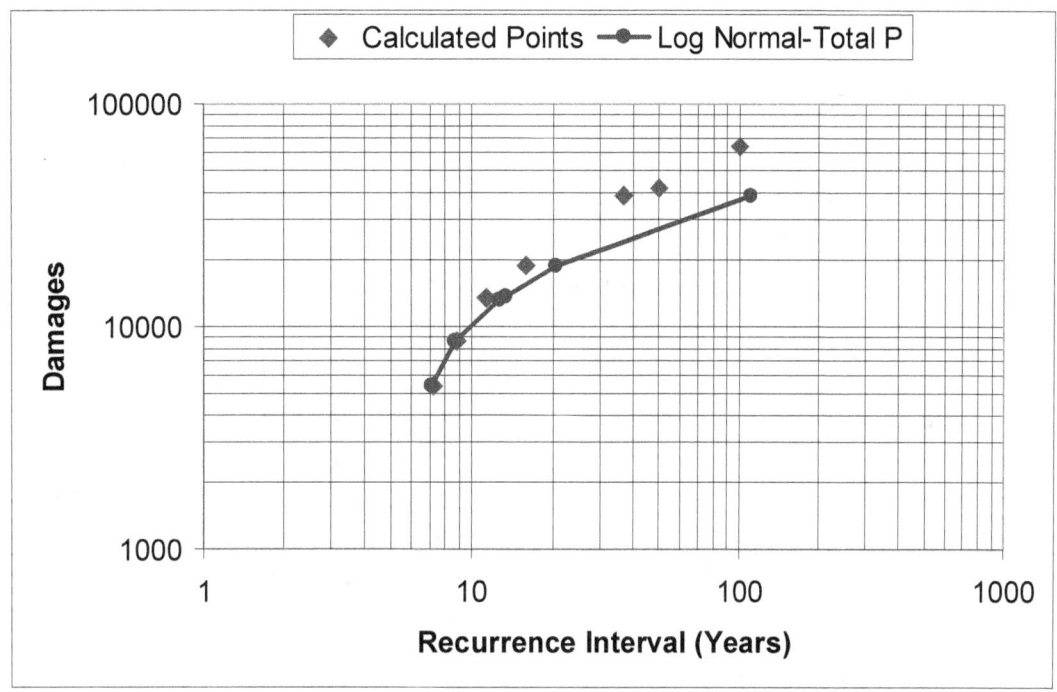

Figure 6. Log-Normal Distribution Plot with Numbers from a Sample Analysis

Damage Value Grouping: In order to avoid too many RI assignments in the final results, the inflated damage values that are relatively close to each other are grouped together and assigned a common RI. As expressed in the formula below, the spreadsheets takes the inflated damage values through four stages of data grouping in which values that are less than 10 percent different from each other are grouped together.

If $[100 \, (\text{IDVURI}_m - \text{IDVURI}_{m+1}) \, / \, (\text{IDVURI}_m)] < 10$ then, group the Damage Values

Where: IDVURI = Inflated Damage Value with Unknown RI (in current dollars)

m = the rank of a given damage value when all IDVURIs are sorted in descending order

When the above condition holds, the log-average of the grouped events is used to represent one damage value for each group and log-average of ranks is used to evaluate one RI for each group, as shown below.

$$\text{m}_{ga} = e^{(0.5(\ln(m)+\ln(m+1)))}$$

$$\text{Grouped IDVURI} = e^{(0.5(\ln(IDVURI_m)+\ln(IDVURI_{m+1})))}$$

Where: m_{ga} = the rank of the event after grouping adjustment

e = exponential,

ln = the natural logarithm.

Probability Adjustment for Years with No Damage: In the next stage, the probabilities calculated for each event are adjusted for the years with no damage. The calculations of this stage are essentially based on total probability theory, but the conditional probabilities are evaluated by dividing the number of events by the period of analysis plus 1 year (Analysis Duration) rather than just the period of analysis. The total probability theorem as applied in the spreadsheet calculations is described in the paragraphs that follow.

The analysis period is divided into two parts: the years with damage and the years without damage (zero-damage years). These two parts are mutually exclusive. In other words, when the user inputs the damage data years and the period of analysis, the user acknowledges that all the years in the period of analysis for which damage is not provided are zero-damage years.

According to the total probability theorem, the probability of zero damages is simply equal to the proportion of zero-damage years to the duration of analysis:

$$P(0) = \frac{k}{n}$$

Where: $P(0)$ = the proportion of zero-damage years over the period of analysis

k = the number of zero damage years (in years)

n = the period of analysis (in years)

The probability of damages (nonzero years) is evaluated using the following conditional formula:

$$P(> 0) = \left[\frac{(n-k)}{n} \right] F(x)$$

Where: $P(>0)$ = the proportion of non zero-damage years over the period of analysis

$F(x)$ is the cumulative probability distribution fitted to the damage data

The total probability distribution is then evaluated as the sum of the two probability terms above. The simple form of the equation for RI adjusted for zero-damage years is shown below:

$$RI = \left[\frac{(n+1)}{(1 - [k + (n-k) F(x)])} \right]$$

Because the number of years with damage (damage events) is typically very small, it is not possible to fit a statistical distribution to the data with a large degree of confidence. The spreadsheet calculations use the ordered statistics combined with grouping and Weiball plotting position adjustment to evaluate $F(x)$ for each inflated damage value. As a side calculation, the spreadsheet also fits a log-normal distribution to the inflated damages to be used for outlier detection and adjustment. Zhang and Singh (2005) identified Normal distribution (after Box-Cox transformation) followed closely by log-normal distribution as best fits to their data for non-zero damage values.

In the spreadsheet, the cumulative probability distribution $F(x)$ is simply calculated as the adjusted rank of the damage event (after grouping) divided by the number of years with damages (adding 1 to the denominator is delayed until after adjustment for zero-damage years):

$$F(x) = \left[\frac{m_{ga}}{(n-k)} \right]$$

The above equations work out such that for the simple cases where no grouping is needed, the calculated RI of each damage event approaches the values calculated by the alternate estimation technique from the FEMA Mitigation BCA Toolkit CD (Version 3.0, July 2006), provided they are not subject to outlier and historical event adjustments as described in the sections that follow.

High Outlier Detection and Adjustment: Next, the spreadsheet checks to detect the presence of a high outlier. A high outlier is a point that has an unknown RI that is potentially longer than the period of record. If the damage data includes no outliers, the largest RI evaluated in the spreadsheet would be equal to the period of analysis plus 1 year. If the highest inflated damage is larger than the upper limit calculated for an outlier, then the RI for that value is calculated using a weighted average between the original RI and the RI from a statistical F-test of log normal fit to the data.

The spreadsheet calculations check the data to detect a high outlier and if detected, adjust the RI for it. The method used is based on tolerance intervals for measurements from a normal distribution; similar to U.S. Geological Survey (USGS) Bulletin 17B. However, because the number of years with damages is usually small, calculations are done directly without the need to look up numbers from tables. The tolerance interval calculations used in the spreadsheet are similar to the technique described on the Engineering Statistics Handbook Web site.

$$IDVURI_u = IDVURI_{avg} + k_1 SD$$

Where: $IDVURI_u$ = the upper limit of inflated damage value beyond which a damage point must be considered as an outlier

$IDVURI_{avg}$ = the inflated average of the damage values

k_1 = a factor determined so that the intervals cover at least a proportion (p) of the population with given level of confidence

SD = the sample standard deviation of the damage data

$$SD = \sqrt{\frac{n\sum_{i=1}^{n} IDVURI^2 - (\sum_{i=1}^{n} IDVURI)^2}{n(n-1)}}$$

If the highest inflated damage is larger than the upper limit calculated for the outlier, then the RI for that value is adjusted to a value larger than n+1 years. The parameters needed for high outlier detection are calculated according to the following equations (Natrella, 1963):

$$k_1 = \left[\frac{z_{1-p} + \sqrt{z_{1-p}^2 - ab}}{a} \right]$$

Where: k = an approximate factor for one-sided tolerance intervals

$$a = 1 - \left[\frac{z_{1-\gamma}^2}{2(N-1)} \right]$$

$$b = z_{1-p}^2 - \left[\frac{z_{1-\gamma}^2}{N} \right]$$

z_{1-p} = the critical value from the normal distribution that is exceeded with probability 1-p

$z_{1-\gamma}$ = the critical value from the normal distribution that is exceeded with probability 1-γ

The value of p is set to 0.1 to allow a 90 percent tolerance, consistent with USGS Bulletin 17B. Unlike the value of p, the value of γ has not been well standardized and may be set by the user. For the case of damage events, repeated calculations were performed to determine an appropriate value for γ. Accordingly, a 50 percent certainty was found to produce reasonable results under most cases tested. Therefore, the value of γ was set to 0.5. Also, the value of N for calculation of a and b was evaluated as the number of non-zero damage values (n-k) because normal distribution parameters are calculated based on only the damage values.

In the absence of any outlier, the largest damage event will have an RI of n+1 years. If the above calculations show that the largest damage value is in fact an outlier, then the RI for that event is adjusted to a weighted average value between RIs estimated by the regular spreadsheet calculations and by fitting a log-normal distribution to the data points and then adjusting the results for total probability. The log-normal distribution tends to assign very large RI values to an outlier due to the small number of observations. The desired RI would be somewhere between n+1 and the RI evaluated by log-normal distribution. The weighting factor is obtained by the value of a statistical F-Test (between 0 and 1.0) that shows how well the variability of the data points is represented by log-normal distribution. This is defined in the spreadsheet using the following Excel formula (FTEST):

FTEST (IDVURIs from data, IDVURIs predicted by log-normal distribution)

Where: FTEST = a test function used to determine whether two samples have different variances (the mathematical function can be found in any standard statistics book). It is displayed in Excel as FTEST(array1, array2) where array 1 is the first array or range of data and array 2 is the second array or range of data.

Each predicted IDVURI is evaluated by using the inverse log function in Excel (LOGINV):

LOGINV(1-(m/(n-k+1), mean ln(IDVURI), SD ln(IDVURI))

Where: LOGINV = a formula that returns the inverse of the log-normal cumulative distribution function of x, where ln(x) is normally distributed with parameters mean and SD. It is displayed in Excel as LOGINV(probability, mean, SD) where probability is a probability associated with the log-normal distribution, mean is the mean of ln(x), and SD is the standard deviation of ln(x).

              mean ln (IDVURI) = the average of natural logarithm of all IDVURIs

              SD ln (IDVURI) = the standard deviation of natural logarithm of all IDVURIs

The F-Test value is evaluated for the inflated data points versus values predicted by the log-normal distribution for the same data set. The better the log-normal distribution fits the data, the larger the weight given to the RI calculated by it (after adjustment for total probability) compared to an RI of n+1. The adjusted RI for outlier (RI_{ao}) is then evaluated using the following Excel formula:

RI_{ao} = (1-FTEST)(RI) + FTEST (RI_{LN})

Where: RI_{ao} = the Recurrence Interval adjusted for a high outlier

              RI_{LN} = the Recurrence Interval from a log normal fit to the original DVURIs adjusted by total probability theory as described previously, except that each DVURI value is replaced by its predicted value from Log-Normal distribution calculated in Excel by:

              LOGNORMDIST(DVURI, mean ln (DVURI), SD ln (DVURI))

16

The end result is usually an RI that is larger than the period of analysis plus 1 year, but smaller than the RI calculated exclusively by log-normal distribution. As shown in Figure 6, a graph in the spreadsheet shows how closely the processed data (damage values subjected to inflation, grouping, conditional probability adjustment, and outlier adjustment) follow log-normal distribution adjusted to total probability.

Historical Events with Known Damages Detection and Adjustment: In the next stage of calculations, the spreadsheet looks for any damages with a known RI in the input section. If historical damages are provided by the user, the spreadsheet will implement an appropriate adjustment to consider such events. The event(s) with a known RI must have happened within the analysis duration (i.e., lifetime of the structure or period of record), but the known RI of the event must exceed the analysis duration. The spreadsheet can handle up to two such events, provided that the inflated damage value for each event is larger than all other inflated damages including any event designated by the spreadsheet as a high outlier. All other damage RIs are adjusted to accommodate the known RIs. If the RI of a high outlier is already adjusted upward, its RI is readjusted to consider both the impact of the historical events and the high outlier.

The adjustment for historical events is based on revising the ranks of the damage events. By entering a known RI that exceeds the structure life (or period of record), the analysis period is extended to the historical period plus 1 year. For example, if a structure was constructed 30 years ago and the user enters damage with a known 100-year RI, then the spreadsheet recalculates all RIs based on a period of analysis of 101 years. Depending on the particulars of a given case, this may increase or decrease the total benefits for the structure in a BCA. At the end of this stage, the adjusted RIs for the events with unknown RIs and the RIs for historical events as provided by the user form a consistent set of frequency-damage values.

To calculate the required adjustment to historical damages, an approach similar to the historic data approach in Appendix 6 of USGS Bulletin 17B is used. The underlying assumption in Bulletin 17B is that the systematic record is representative of the intervening period between the systematic record and historic record length. However, in case of the damage frequency problem, the historical event actually happens within the systematic record period (otherwise a damage is not recorded for the structure in question). Unlike Bulletin 17B, the event RI estimations in the spreadsheet are not directly based on any standard statistical distribution and no distribution parameter adjustment is needed.

Instead, the RIs for all IDVURIs are adjusted directly to accommodate the known RIs.

The adjustment for historical events is based on revising the ranks of the damage events when the damages are ranked from largest to smallest. The one (or two) historical event is ranked as number one (or number one and two). The rank of the other inflated and grouped damages are revised by the following equation:

$R_r = W R - (W-1) (Z+0.5)$

Where: R_r = the revised rank

              R = the original rank

              Z = the number of historical damages with known RI (limited to two in the spreadsheet)

              W = the weight of the historical event and is calculated by:

$$W = \frac{H - Z}{N}$$

              Where: H = the larger of the two RIs for damages with known RI and

              N = the period of analysis in years (included number of years with damage plus years without damage)

If there was an outlier adjustment, only for the outlier damage, the new rank would be Z plus a revised rank which would be less than 1 and is calculated by the ratio of the period of analysis to the RI_{ao}.

Next, the revised RI (RI_r) is calculated for each event by the following equation:

$$RI_r = \frac{(H+1)}{R_r}$$

Note that the above equation is only applied to events with unknown RI. The one (or two) damage with known RI keeps its RI as input by the user and controls the RI of every other event. Therefore, it is extremely important to use an event(s) with known RI only if the RI is from a credible source with a high degree of confidence and the underlying mechanism causing the historical damage is the same as all other damage events considered. By entering a known RI that exceeds structure life (or period for which data is available), the analysis period is extended to the historical period. If these conditions are not met, the user can simply input the historical event(s) as any other IDVURI and let the spreadsheet evaluate an RI for it.

Output Section: At the end of the calculation process, all inflated damages subject to the above grouping and adjustments are sorted in ascending order and the final results consisting of RI-inflated damage pairs are displayed in the spreadsheet output section. The values in the output section may be transferred to the LD Module to estimate the project benefits. Figure 7 shows the final results of the sample analysis in Figure 5 as listed in the output section of the spreadsheet. Note that unlike historical damage values reported in dollars, the loss of service calculations are not subject to inflation to the analysis year.

INPUT							Results	
Analysis Year (4 digit year)	Year Built (4 digit year)	Analysis Duration (years)	User Input Analysis Duartion (years)				Upper Limit for Inflated Damage Outlier	Adjustment of Tr for outlier applied?
2007	1970	38					$31,498	Yes
Historical Damage Data							Recurrence Interval (Tr) (years)	Damages (dollars)
Damages with Unknown Recurrence Interval			Damages with Known Recurrence Interval					
Damage Year (4 digit year)	Total damage (dollars)	Damages inflated to analysis Year (dollars)	Damage Year (4 digit year)	Total damage (dollars)	Known Recurrence Interval (years)	Damages inflated to analysis Year (dollars)	7.2	$5,373
							8.8	$8,609
1974	$9,000	$38,626	1971	$12,200	100	$63,724	11.3	$13,408
1989	$8,000	$13,647	1980	$16,200	50	$41,583	15.9	$18,630
1991	$12,000	$18,630	User Notes:				36.7	$38,626
1997	$10,000	$13,174					50.0	$41,583
2000	$7,000	$8,609					100.0	$63,724
2001	$4,500	$5,373						

Figure 7. Results in the Spreadsheet Output Section from a Sample Analysis

A flow diagram of the revised statistical analysis technique to determining unknown frequencies is provided in Figure 8.

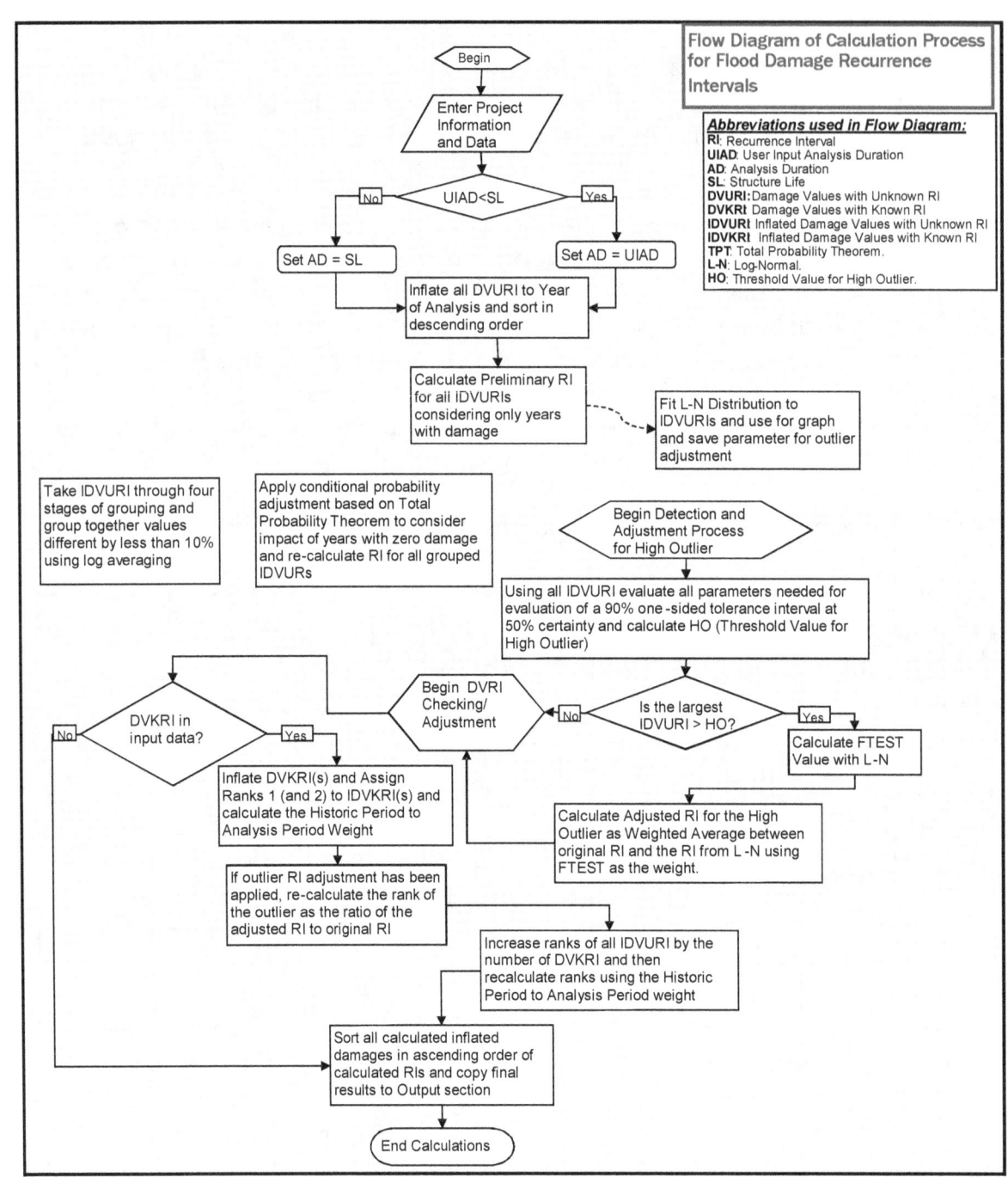

Figure 8. Flow Diagram for Revised Statistical Analysis Technique to Determine Unknown Frequencies

20

Comparison of Alternative Methodologies and Solution to Address Problem Statement 1

A comparison of the two alternative methodologies is provided in Table 1. A review of Table 1 indicates that although methodology 1 is supported by the 2006 FEMA Mitigation BCA Toolkit guidance, methodology 2 provides greater flexibility in application and accounts for more statistical anomalies in the historic hazard data. For this reason, further development of the revised statistical analysis technique (methodology 2) was recommended to automatically and consistently determine unknown frequencies in the LD Module.

Table 1. Comparison of Alternate Methodologies to Address Problem Statement 1 (Determine Unknown Frequencies)

Item	Methodology 1: Automate Alternate Estimation Technique	Methodology 2: Establish Revised Statistical Analysis Technique
Methodology supported by the 2006 FEMA Mitigation BCA Toolkit guidance	Yes	No
Methodology supported by statistical analysis and academic research	No	Yes
Spreadsheet does not use macros to facilitate use in BCAR programming initiative	No	Yes
Accounts for statistical anomalies in data (high outliers)	No	Yes
Accounts for known event frequencies if available	No	Yes
Adjusts results for years within period of record when no event(s) occurred	No	Yes

In September 2007, the BCAR Technical Advisory Group (TAG) endorsed methodology 2 for determining unknown frequency events in the LD Module, known hereafter as the unknown frequency calculator. Following the September TAG Meeting, the updated

FEMA BCA Inflation Calculator was incorporated into the unknown frequency calculator (refer to Problem Statement 2 for details).

Note that in the latest version of the software, the input interface has been expanded and refined based on initial user feedback to input up to five damage categories and up to three road/utility service losses.

Problem Statement 2: Update the FEMA Inflation Calculator and Include in the LD Module

The FEMA LD Module for BCA requires all historic damage events and losses to be inflated to the present value in order to calculate project benefits. However, the LD Module does not have the ability to automatically inflate historic damages to the present value.

In order to address this problem, FEMA developed an inflation calculator for the FEMA Mitigation BCA Toolkit CD (Version 3.0, July 2006) that can be used to update historic damages to the present value for input into the LD Module. The FEMA Inflation Calculator on Version 3.0 of the BCA Toolkit CD could update up to five historic damage values to the present value based on the Consumer Price Index (CPI) for damages prior to 1999 and a 3.0 percent annual inflation rate for damages after 1999.

Although the FEMA Inflation Calculator addressed some of the difficulties associated with updating historic damages for inflation, problems with updating historic damages for inflation persisted for the following reasons:

1. The FEMA Inflation Calculator did not provide a defensible methodology for the 3.0 percent annual inflation rate used between 1999 and the present. The calculator does allow users to override the 3.0 percent annual inflation rate for 1999 and replace with a CPI value, but no guidance is provided on how to accomplish this.

2. The current calculator could only handle five values at a time.

3. The FEMA Inflation Calculator results had to be transferred manually from the calculator to the LD Module.

4. The calculator and the LD Module could not be opened at the same time without losing the custom menu bar in the LD Module.

Based on feedback from BCA applicants and users, there was a need to develop and automate a standard methodology to consistently update historic damage events and losses for inflation within the LD Module.

Methodology to Address Problem Statement 2

In September 2007, the URS BCA Team developed a revised FEMA Inflation Calculator, which allowed historic damage events to be updated for inflation to the present value by selecting one of two established inflation indexes: the CPI or the Engineering News Record (ENR). The URS BCA Team originally envisioned that the ENR could be used to update building damages and other reconstruction costs, while the CPI could be used to update contents damages. However, based on BCAR TAG discussions in September 2007, it was agreed that for the sake of clarity and consistency, the ENR inflation index be used for both building and contents damages.

After the revised FEMA Inflation Calculator was modified to reflect the recommendations of the September TAG, it was incorporated into the unknown frequency calculator for ease of use. Since that time, the URS BCA Team has incorporated the following methodology to address problem statement 2:

1. Incorporate the modified FEMA Inflation Calculator into the unknown frequency calculator so that historic damages and losses for unknown frequency events are automatically updated for inflation to the present value.

2. Incorporate the modified FEMA Inflation Calculator into a new input interface for the LD Module so that historic damages and losses for known frequency events are automatically updated for inflation to the present value.

3. Include a toggle box into a new input interface to allow users to input values that have already been inflated without using the modified FEMA Inflation Calculator.

Problem Statement 3: Improve Guidance on Use of the LD Module

In September 2007, the BCAR TAG endorsed the unknown frequency calculator methodology recommended by the URS BCA Team for determining unknown frequency events in the LD Module (refer to Problem Statement 1 for additional details.) Following the September TAG Meeting, the URS BCA Team met with URS programmers in October 2007 to discuss "storyboarding" of the unknown frequency calculator and the LD Module. During the September TAG meeting and the October URS storyboarding meeting, the following discussion issues/questions were raised regarding the unknown frequency calculator:

1. What period of record should be used when determining event frequencies using the unknown frequency calculator? What is the minimum period of record needed to use the unknown frequency calculator?

2. What is the minimum number of historic events needed to use the unknown frequency calculator?

3. What are the recommendations for interpolation between two or more known hazard events?

4. What are the recommendations for extrapolation beyond two or more known hazard events?

5. Can the methodology used in the unknown frequency calculator be applied to non-flood hazard events?

As a result of these discussions, the URS BCA Team investigated these issues further and provided methodologies to improve guidance for the unknown frequency calculator/LD Module for the period of record, number of historic events, use of interpolation and extrapolation, and the applicability of the unknown frequency calculator methodology for non-flood hazards.

Methodologies to Address Problem Statement 3

Period of Record

The period of record can be defined as the length of time in years that records are kept for historic damages, losses, or hazard levels (e.g., flood elevations or wind speeds). When the frequencies of hazard events are unknown, the period of record is essential to determining event frequencies. However, when the frequencies of hazard events are known (i.e., supported by documentation), the period of record is not needed to use the frequency-damage assessment in the LD Module. The unknown frequency calculator assumes the period of record to be a single, uninterrupted length of time; so if no damages/losses are recorded for a given year within the period, then no hazard events occurred that year. While this may not be a completely accurate assumption, in a statistical analysis of annual events, small data gaps within the period can generally be ignored.

Ideally, the period of record should equal the age of the building or facility that is being mitigated. Although the period of insurance has been used previously, this is not considered acceptable because it is typically shorter than the age of the structure and may not reflect the true hazard history at the site. In the absence of any information to the contrary, the new unknown frequency calculator performs a statistical analysis based on the age of the structure plus 1 year, and excludes any events that occurred prior to year the structure was built (refer to Problem Statement 1 for additional details). However, as demonstrated in the following scenarios, the age of the structure can sometimes be difficult to use as the period of record because:

1. Most newly constructed structures do not have sufficient records of damages/losses due to their limited age.

2. Many older structures do not have complete records of damages/losses that extend back to the date of construction. In some cases, such as floods, the available damage/loss data may suggest a significant change in local flow conditions in recent years, which may indicate a need to adjust the period of record.

25

To address these situations, an alternate means for determining the period of record needed to be established.

As stated in the previous paragraph, the age of the structure that is being mitigated should typically be used as the period of record. The alternate estimation technique for determining unknown frequencies on the BCA Mitigation Toolkit CD (Version 3.0, July 2006) specified a minimum required time period of at least 5 years. However, for the unknown frequency calculator, a period of record of at least 30 years is preferred as the time period to conduct a thorough statistical analysis. Therefore, in an effort to provide a balance between the applicant's need for a reasonable time period for maintaining records and the calculator's need for a sufficient time period to produce a decent analysis, the period of record input into the unknown frequency calculator should equal the age of the structure, or a minimum of 10 years, whichever is greater. This methodology may be used to address the first scenario of newly constructed structures (i.e., structures less than 10 years old).

For the second scenario, where older structures have experienced a change in local flow conditions, the age of the structure should be used as the period of record unless the applicant can provide the following documentation: 1) an analysis by a hydrologist/engineer demonstrating that the local flow conditions have changed, and 2) statistical tests, such as a T-Test, confirming that the change in flow conditions was statistically significant. If the applicant can satisfy these requirements, then the period of record can be assumed to begin on the date when the change first occurred. Another option to consider to address this situation (if the requirements listed above are met) is to use the age of the structure for the period of record, but adjust the historic flood hazard event data using statistical tools, such as a double-mass curve.

Number of Historic Events

A historic event can be defined as an actual recorded damage, service loss, or hazard level (e.g., flood depth or wind speed) occurring at the structure being mitigated. When the frequencies of hazard events are known (i.e., supported by documentation), a minimum of two historic events are required to use the LD Module. As an exception to this requirement, a single historic event of known frequency may be used to run the LD Module, provided that additional supporting documentation is provided that includes the age of the structure. In addition, a BCA based on only one historic event does not produce a best-data analysis, and no interpolation or extrapolation of additional damages or losses is permitted.

When the frequencies of hazard events are unknown, a minimum of three historic events is required to use the new unknown frequency calculator in the LD Module, and all of the events must occur within the period of record specified by the applicant. This is because the unknown frequency calculator detects and adjusts for high outliers by plotting a log-normal distribution, and a minimum of three data points are necessary to plot an accurate curve. The methodology requirement is also consistent with the guidance provided for the alternate estimation technique for determining unknown frequencies on the BCA Mitigation Toolkit CD (Version 3.0, July 2006), which specifies a minimum of three historic flood/hazard events. The only exception to this requirement is when one or two historic events within the period of record have known frequencies. In this case, the applicant can input a minimum of two additional hazard events in the unknown frequency calculator.

Interpolation

Interpolation involves the estimation of additional historic event damages and/or losses that occur between two or more known historic event damages and/or losses. Current FEMA BCA guidance permits interpolation between two or more documented, historic events. However, the current BCA guidance does not provide any clear methodology on how to perform this interpolation. As a result, LD Module users must manually interpolate between known events using linear interpolations or some other form of engineering judgment that often produces inconsistent results. In an effort to address this problem, the unknown frequency calculator and the revised LD Module have been programmed with a calculator to automatically interpolate between hazard event damages and losses input by the user. The methodology used to conduct the automated interpolation calculation is described in Appendix A of this report, and allows users to obtain BCA results that are more consistent and accurate. There are no exceptions to the requirement for using the automated calculation methodology for interpolation in the unknown frequency calculator or the revised LD Module.

Extrapolation

Extrapolation involves the estimation of additional historic event damages and/or losses that occur beyond two or more known historic event damages and/or losses. Current FEMA BCA guidance does not permit extrapolation of less frequent (larger) events or more frequent (smaller) events beyond two or more documented, historic events. This was indicated on page 17 of the *Flood Data Derivation* guidance document on the FEMA BCA Mitigation Toolkit CD (Version 3.0 dated July 2006); which states:

> "Flood frequency estimates may be developed based on **an interpolation between known data points**, but users **should not extrapolate above or below the known data points**."

However, other BCA experts contend that while extrapolation of more frequent (smaller) events should be prohibited, extrapolation of less frequent (larger) events beyond two or more documented, historic events may be justified under certain circumstances. For example, if a building has historic damages from documented 10-year and 25-year flood events, and the mitigation project will be to elevate the structure to provide protection up to the 100-year flood event, then it seems reasonable to permit extrapolation of the 10-year and 25-year flood event damages to the 50-year event if the flood depth can be determined from the FEMA Flood Insurance Study (FIS) and damages can be predicted based on a Depth-Damage Function (DDF) relationship.

The URS BCA Team investigated the possibility of using extrapolation to estimate less frequent (larger) events beyond two or more documented, historic events. For the unknown frequency calculator, any extrapolation of event damages/losses is not feasible because there are no frequencies associated with the damage/loss events input by the user. For the LD Module, experience has shown that the vast majority of extrapolated event damages/losses have little or no impact on the final BCA result for the following reasons:

1. Extrapolated event damages/losses add only minimal benefits because they are estimated for events that occur less frequently than the documented, historic events in the BCA.

2. Extrapolated event damages/losses add only minimal benefits because most extrapolated damages/losses before mitigation will be reduced by extrapolated damages/losses after mitigation.

3. Extrapolated event damages before mitigation generally do not add significant benefits because they are limited to the replacement value of the building or facility that is being mitigated.

4. Extrapolated event losses before mitigation generally do not add benefits because FEMA's What Is a Benefit? guidance values for loss of road or utility service cannot be used where loss of service times are estimated. As a result, extrapolated event service losses using the guidance values must either be capped at the maximum loss of service from documented, historic events, or the guidance values must be replaced with the documented annual operating budget of the facility.

Therefore, the URS BCA Team has concluded that extrapolated event damages/losses should not be considered when using the unknown frequency calculator and the revised LD Module. There are only two exceptions to this prohibition. The first exception is if two or more historic events with known (documented) frequencies are available. Extrapolation of less frequent (larger) events is permitted, provided the damages do not exceed documented facility/contents replacement values and service losses are based on the documented annual operating budget for the facility. The second exception is for expected damages and losses based on documented engineering estimates.

Application of Unknown Frequency Calculator Methodology to Non-Flood Hazard Events

The unknown frequency calculator methodology (i.e., alternate methodology 2 to address problem statement 1) was developed for flood events based on flood guidance from USGS Bulletin 17B and Zhang and Singh (2005). However, a review of hazard statistics indicates that flood events tend to follow the same basic frequency-damage relationship as most other natural hazards, such as where the frequency of hazard events decreases (and the recurrence interval increases) as the magnitude of the damage increases. Therefore, the URS BCA Team has concluded that the unknown frequency methodology can be applied to most non-flood hazard events, including winter storms, high wind events, and earthquakes. The one exception to this conclusion would be for one-time, non-recurring hazard events, such as landslides, which do not generally conform to the same frequency-damage relationship as floods and other natural hazards.

Recommendations to Address Problem Statement 3:

The URS BCA Team's recommended methodologies for using the unknown frequency calculator is summarized in the guidance in Table 2 on page 28. Recommended methodologies for the LD Module (where frequencies are known and supported by documentation) is summarized in the guidance in Table 3 on page 29.

29

Table 2. Summary of Guidance for the Unknown Frequency Calculator

Parameter	Guidance Requirement for Parameter	Exceptions to Guidance Requirement
Period of Record	Input the age of the structure or a minimum of 10 years, whichever is greater.	For older structures where flood damage/loss data indicate a significant change in local flow conditions, the period of record can be assumed to begin on the date when the change first occurred, if the applicant can document that 1) local flow conditions have changed based on hydrologist/ engineering analysis, and 2) the change in flow conditions was statistically significant based on statistical tests (e.g., T-Test). Another option if requirements 1 and 2 are met is to use the age of the structure as the period of record, but adjust the historic event data using statistical techniques (e.g., double-mass curve).
Number of Historic Events	Input a minimum of three events within the specified period of record.	Only two additional hazard events are required if the applicant can provide one or two historic events within the period of record with known frequencies.
Interpolation Between Known Hazard Events	Interpolation permitted between two or more known hazard events, using automated calculation methodology in revised LD Module (Appendix A).	None
Extrapolation Beyond Known Hazard Events	Extrapolation is not permitted.	None
Unknown Frequency	Methodology is applicable	Methodology not applicable for

Parameter	Guidance Requirement for Parameter	Exceptions to Guidance Requirement
Methodology for Non-Flood Hazard Events	for most non-flood hazard events.	one-time, non-recurring hazard events (e.g., landslides).

Table 3. Summary of Guidance for Using the LD Module[1]

Parameter	Guidance Requirement for Parameter	Exceptions to Guidance Requirement
Period of Record	Not Applicable	Not Applicable
Number of Historic Events	Input a minimum of two events.	One known historic event may be used if additional supporting documentation is provided that includes the age of the structure. Note that a BCA based on only one historic event does not produce a best-data analysis, and no interpolation or extrapolation of additional damages or losses is permitted.
Interpolation Between Known Hazard Events	Interpolation permitted between two or more known hazard events, using automated calculation methodology in revised LD Module (Appendix A).	One known historic event may be used as a screening tool if the age of structure is documented
Extrapolation Beyond Known Hazard Events	Extrapolation is not permitted.	Extrapolation of less frequent (larger) damage events is permitted beyond two or more known hazard events, provided the damages do not exceed documented facility/contents replacement values. Extrapolation of less frequent (larger) loss events is permitted beyond two or more known hazard events, provided the service losses are based on the documented annual operating budget for the facility. Extrapolation is also permitted for expected damages and losses based on documented engineering estimates.

Parameter	Guidance Requirement for Parameter	Exceptions to Guidance Requirement
Unknown Frequency Methodology for Non-Flood Hazard Events	Not Applicable	Not Applicable

Note: 1) The frequency of all historic events is assumed to be known when using the LD Module; otherwise, the unknown frequency calculator must be used and the minimum requirements in Table 2 apply.

Problem Statement 4: Improve Guidance on After-Mitigation Damages for the LD Module

Mitigation is defined as an action specifically taken to reduce or eliminate future damages and losses from the hazard that is being addressed. Although a few hazard mitigation projects, such as acquisition, eliminate all future damages and losses, the majority of hazard mitigation projects reduce the amount of damage, but do not eliminate damage. The FEMA LD Module for BCA requires the user to input historic event damages and losses before mitigation based on documented, historic events. Since most hazard mitigation projects do not eliminate all future damages, the user also must estimate event damages and losses after mitigation in order to determine the project benefits (i.e., the difference between the damages and losses before mitigation and those after mitigation). Unfortunately, neither the current LD Module nor the current BCA guidance provide any clear guidance on how to estimate damages and losses after mitigation. As a result, many LD Module users either do not input any damages after mitigation or attempt to incorrectly estimate damages after mitigation; which can produce inconsistent or inaccurate results depending on the type of mitigation project being analyzed. Therefore, based on this information and feedback from BCA applicants and users, there is a need to develop and automate a standard methodology to consistently estimate damages after mitigation for the most common projects analyzed using the LD Module.

Proposed Methodology Recommendations to Address Problem Statement 4
In an effort to address this problem, the URS BCA Team was directed to develop improved guidance on estimating after-mitigation damages and losses. The first step in estimating after-mitigation damages and losses is to determine the anticipated level of protection that will be provided by the mitigation. A review of current BCA guidance indicates that there is insufficient information available on how to document the level of

protection. As a result, the first need identified by the team was to provide users with improved guidance on documenting the anticipated level of protection provided by the mitigation project.

The URS BCA Team initially worked to see if a simplified method could be developed to estimate after-mitigation damages and losses for various mitigation project types based on the before-mitigation damages/losses and the level of protection input into the unknown frequency calculator or the LD Module. However, initial analysis revealed that an engineering analysis of the after-mitigation conditions was needed to accurately determine after-mitigation damages and losses. Therefore, it was decided to provide guidance to estimate after-mitigation damages in the absence of an engineering analysis based on before-mitigation damages and the level of protection.

The URS BCA Team's proposed recommended methodology for estimating damages after mitigation based on damages before mitigation and the level of protection in the unknown frequency calculator/LD Module is summarized in the guidance in Table 4 on pages 31 and 32. Note that the URS BCA Team was unable to implement the methodology recommendations in Table 4 into the unknown frequency calculator and the LD Module. However, it is anticipated that the methodology recommendations will be finalized and implemented in some future revision to the BCAR software.

Table 4. Summary of Proposed Guidance to Address Problem Statement 4
(Estimate After-Mitigation Damages For the LD Module)

Hazard	Mitigation Project Type	Estimated Damages/Losses After Mitigation		Basic Assumptions
		Up to Level of Protection	At/Beyond Level of Protection	
Flood	Acquisition/ Relocation	None	None	Acquired/relocated facility is moved outside the 500-year floodplain
Flood	Elevation	None	Use lowest before-mitigation damages/ losses beginning at level of protection	Facilities are typically elevated to the 100-year flood elevation plus 1 foot of freeboard
Flood	Culverts/Drainage Control Projects	None	Use same before-mitigation damages/losses beginning at level of protection	Conservative assumption when no post-mitigation hydraulics and hydrology analysis is

Hazard	Mitigation Project Type	Estimated Damages/Losses After Mitigation		Basic Assumptions
		Up to Level of Protection	At/Beyond Level of Protection	
				available
Flood	Dry Floodproofing/ Barriers (Floodwalls or Levees)	None	Use same before-mitigation damages/losses beginning at level of protection	No protection provided by flood barriers once the design capacity is reached
Flood	Wet Floodproofing	Use before-mitigation damages reduced by 50%	Use same before-mitigation damages/losses beginning at level of protection	Wet floodproofing will reduce damage, but cleanup costs will remain
Wind	Shutters	Use before-mitigation damages reduced by 50% or consider use of after-mitigation Wind Damage Functions (WDFs) from the Hurricane Wind Module	Use same before-mitigation damages/losses beginning at level of protection	Shutters will reduce contents damages, but other damages will remain
Wind	Structural Retrofit	Use before-mitigation damages reduced by 75% or consider use of after-mitigation WDFs from the Hurricane Wind Module	Use same before-mitigation damages/losses beginning at level of protection	Structural wind retrofit will provide better protection than shutters alone
Wind	Burying Utility Lines	Use before-mitigation damages reduced by 75%	Use minimal before-mitigation damages/ losses beginning at level of protection	Utility lines buried for short distances subject to frequent wind damage
Earthquake	Structural Retrofit	Use before-mitigation damages reduced by 75%	Use same before-mitigation damages/ losses beginning at level of protection	Structural earthquake retrofit will provide limited protection

References

1. "Engineering Statistics Handbook Web Page, NIST/Sematech Handbook,"
   Section 7.2.6.3
   (http://www.itl.nist.gov/div898/handbook/prc/section2/prc263.htm)

2. "Flood Data Derivation," FEMA Mitigation BCA Toolkit CD, Version 3.0, July 2006,
   Section 1.5.3.

3. Mary Gibbons Natrella, 1963. "Experimental Statistics", National Bureau of
   Standards (NBS Handbook 91), US Department of Commerce, Washington, DC.

4. USGS Bulletin 17B, Interagency Advisory Committee of Water Data, 1982.
   "Guidelines for Determining Flood Flow Frequency," U.S. Geological Survey,
   Reston, VA.

5. Zhang, L. and Singh, V.J. (2005) "Frequency Analysis of Flood Damages," ASCE
   Journal of Hydrologic Engineering, Vol. 10, No. 2, March 1, 2005, pp. 100-109.

Appendix A: Revision of the Annualized Benefit Calculations in the Limited Data Module

Introduction

The calculations of annualized damages in the 2006 version of the LD Module (Version 5.2.3 dated May 2, 2006) were based on log-linear interpolation of the damage-RI data. No extrapolation below or above the first and last damage values were implemented. For most common situations, this procedure provided reasonable results. However, the calculation method was difficult to justify, to follow, and to model in the new modeling framework of BCAR. The URS BCA Team was not able to verify its theoretical integrity independently. More importantly, the current calculation method led to unreasonable results under certain circumstances. Moreover, the calculation structure of the current method was neither fully compatible with the format of the results from the unknown frequency calculator developed in BCAR nor compatible with the method implemented in the new Flood Full Data (FD) Module for calculation of annualized benefits. This report explains the development of a revised calculation method of annualized benefits for the LD Module that overcomes the problems with the current method.

Revisions to the Current Method

The revised calculation method has a simpler computational structure than the 2006 LD Module solution method. The details and formulas of the new method as implemented in an Excel Spreadsheet are presented in pages that follow.

Because the damages calculated in the LD Module have a lower limit (no interpolation of damages below the lowest declared damage is performed), the results are very sensitive to the values declared for frequent (1-5 year) damages. The 2006 LD Module overestimated the benefits of a mitigation project that eliminates the damages from a small but frequent event. The frequent and recurring damages are sometimes caused by a different mechanism than larger damages (e.g., shallow flooding due to inadequate drainage versus riverine flooding). The revised calculation method decreases the impact of small but frequent damages, but the annualized damages calculated by the revised calculations for larger RIs closely approximates the LD Module results. Furthermore, for all RIs in the calculation table with no damage value (damages repeated from a previous row), the annualized damage calculated by the two methods is identical.

The advantages of implementing the new calculation method over the 2006 method are as follows:

1. The new method is easy to understand and easy to program and modify in the programming language to be used in the new BCAR BCA Module.

2. The estimation of the average damage between any two consecutive data points is consistent with the method used in the new unknown frequency calculation method.

3. The new calculation method prevents overestimation of the benefits of small but frequent damages by using the log average of damage values in calculation of the benefits under the damage-frequency curve. This prevents overestimation of the BCR of small mitigation projects that eliminate damages from small but recurring events (see Example 1 below).

4. The new method allows for the flexibility of using different RI values for after-mitigation compared to before-mitigation. This helps to more accurately reflect the after-mitigation damages when the mitigation is effective up to an RI not used in the before-mitigation data sets and eliminates the manual intervention on the part of the user that makes results subjective to the user choices. Also, the after-mitigation RI damage values developed in an engineering report independently from the before-mitigation data can easily be used.

5. The new method allows blank rows with no data under the row with the largest damage without causing any errors. The current module requires the RI column to be filled for all rows otherwise a division by zero error occurs and no results are given. This fits into the programming plan in which the RI-damage data is automatically input into the LD Module from the unknown frequency calculator.

6. The revised spreadsheet increases the number of before- and after-mitigation damage events from 9 to 12. This allows the revised calculations to accommodate the rare cases in which the combination of multiple types of facilities and a long history of damages would result in more than 9 levels of damages to be considered. The unknown frequency calculator has the potential of producing up to 14 points (12 damage events with calculated RIs plus up to 2 events with given RIs). However, in practice it is very unlikely that 14 damage data points will be used. Furthermore, the damage-grouping operation in the unknown frequency calculator is very likely to reduce the number of data points for cases with a large number of historical damage values. Therefore, 12 rows of calculation would practically cover all cases. Of course this number can easily be increased to 14 in the final BCAR computer modeling.

7. The new method replaces the terminology of "Flood Frequency Events, (Years)" with "Hazard Recurrence Interval, (Years)" to be technically accurate and avoid the confusion and errors associated with the current LD Module.

The revised calculation method, as well as other changes discussed above (e.g., number of calculation rows, label corrections, etc.) were implemented in the LD Module spreadsheet to generate a revised LD Module to be used in BCAR developments.

Example 1 - A Sample BCA by the Two Methods

Example 1 illustrates a small local drainage improvement project with a mitigation cost of $10,000 and project useful life of 50 years. Every other year, heavy rain causes shallow flooding with minimal damages ($1 used here for the 2-year damages to better illustrate the point). Larger damages (10-year and larger RI) are related to riverine flooding. Figure A-1, which is a snap shot of the 2006 version of the LD Module, shows that if the mitigation project results in eliminating the $1 damage associated with the 2-year event (see damages after mitigation), the annual damages decrease from $5,431 to $3,913 (making the BCR of this project 2.09). This conclusion is clearly unreasonable. This case shows that the 2006 LD Module overestimated the impact of eliminating a small but frequent damage event. For this example, if the 2-year event is also a riverine flood causing $10,000 damage before mitigation and $6,000 after mitigation, the BCR is 1.65. In this case, the mitigation reduces the 2-year damage by $4,000 but the BCR is smaller than when it reduced it only by $1.

DAMAGES BEFORE MITIGATION							

Flood Frequency Events (Years)	Scenario Flood Damages			Loss of Function Time and Dollars		TOTAL Damages and Losses	
	A	B	C	Days	Losses	Losses	
2	$1				$0	$1	
10	$15,000				$0	$15,000	
25	$25,000				$0	$25,000	
50	$90,000				$0	$90,000	
60					$0	$90,000	
70					$0	$90,000	
120					$0	$90,000	
150					$0	$90,000	
300					$0	$90,000	
				Total Annualized Damages			$5,431

DAMAGES AFTER MITIGATION							

Flood Frequency Events (Years)	Scenario Flood Damages			Loss of Function Time and Dollars		TOTAL Damages and Losses	
	A	B	C	Days	Losses	Losses	
2	0				$0	$0	
10	15000				$0	$15,000	
25	25000				$0	$25,000	
50	90000				$0	$90,000	
60					$0	$90,000	
70					$0	$90,000	
120					$0	$90,000	
150					$0	$90,000	
300					$0	$90,000	
				Total Annualized Damages			$3,913

Data Sources and Documentation

SUMMARY OF BENEFITS AND COSTS		
	Expected Annual	Present Value
Expected Annual Damages Before Mitigation	$5,431	$74,952
Expected Annual Damages After Mitigation	$3,913	$54,003
Expected Avoided Damages After Mitigation (BENEFITS)	$1,518	$20,949
PROJECT COSTS	$10,000	
PROJECT BENEFITS	$20,949	
BENEFITS MINUS COSTS	$10,949	
BENEFIT-COST RATIO	2.09	

Figure A-1: Example 1 Solved in the 2006 LD Module

Figure A-2 shows the snapshot from the revised calculation spreadsheet solving the same example. As seen in Figure A-2, the revised calculation produces reasonable results for this case. The before-mitigation annual damages are $3,960 and eliminating the 2-year damages only slightly decreases the annual damages to $3,911. The BCR of this mitigation project is only 0.07. If the 2-year damage is reduced from $10,000 before-mitigation to $6,000 post-mitigation the project BCR is 1.52.

DAMAGES BEFORE MITIGATION

Flood Recurrence Interval (Years)	Scenario Flood Damages			Loss of Function Time and Dollars		TOTAL Damages and Losses
	A	B	C	Days	Losses	
2	$1				$0	$1
10	$15,000				$0	$15,000
25	$25,000				$0	$25,000
50	$90,000				$0	$90,000
80					$0	$90,000
100					$0	$90,000
120					$0	$90,000
150					$0	$90,000
300					$0	$90,000
400					$0	$90,000
500					$0	$90,000
600					$0	$90,000
					Total Annualized Damages	$3,960

DAMAGES AFTER MITIGATION

Flood Recurrence Interval (Years)	Scenario Flood Damages			Loss of Function Time and Dollars		TOTAL Damages and Losses
	A	B	C	Days	Losses	
2	$0				$0	$0
10	$15,000				$0	$15,000
25	$25,000				$0	$25,000
50	$90,000				$0	$90,000
80					$0	$90,000
100					$0	$90,000
120					$0	$90,000
150					$0	$90,000
300					$0	$90,000
400					$0	$90,000
500					$0	$90,000
600					$0	$90,000
					Total Annualized Damages	$3,911

SUMMARY OF BENEFITS AND COSTS

	Expected Annual	Present Value
Expected Annual Damages Before Mitigation	$3,960	$54,645
Expected Annual Damages After Mitigation	$3,911	$53,969
Expected Avoided Damages After Mitigation (BENEFITS)	$49	$676

PROJECT COSTS	$10,000
PROJECT BENEFITS	$676
BENEFITS MINUS COSTS	($9,324)
BENEFIT-COST RATIO	0.07

Figure A-2: Example 1 Solved in the Revised LD Module

Notice that in the 2006 LD Module, all the rows with flood frequencies must be populated with increasing RI values. For example, if any of the numbers from 60 to 300 years in the first column of the table shown in Figure 1 are not provided or are not in ascending order, then the spreadsheet produces an error. The revised spreadsheet does not require any RI in addition to the values for which the damages have been determined. This makes a direct interface to pre-calculated RI-damage data sets practical.

The above example outlines a case for which the revised calculations lead to drastically different results from the 2006 LD Module. For most common cases, however, the revised calculation results are going to be very close to the results obtained by the 2006 LD Module. For example, for the case in Example 1 if the 2-year pre-mitigation damage is zero and the mitigation project eliminates the 10-year damage, the LD Module produces a BCR of 1.53 and the revised calculation spreadsheet produces a BCR of 1.60. The revised spreadsheet calculates three more annualized benefits (400-, 500-, and 600-year values) but the sum of these three numbers added to the value calculated for the 300-year add up to the same value that the LD Module calculates for "Flood Frequency Range > 300 years."

Calculation Details - Revised Method

This section summarizes the calculation details in the revised calculation method for evaluating the total annualized benefits as programmed in an Excel Spreadsheet. The calculations are explained with reference to the spreadsheet snapshot in Figure A-3. Figure A-4 shows the same spreadsheet section with cell formulas exposed.

	Flood Recurrence Interval (Years)	Expected Annual No. of Events	TOTAL Damages and Losses	Annualized Damages And Losses
292				
293				
294				
295				
296				
297	10	0.1000	12878	662
298	15	0.0667	30648	1598
299	30	0.0333	75000	2500
300		0.0000	75000	0
301		0.0000	75000	0
302		0.0000	75000	0
303		0.0000	75000	0
304		0.0000	75000	0
305		0.0000	75000	0
306		0.0000	75000	0
307		0.0000	75000	0
308		0.0000	75000	0
309	9999999	0.0000	75000	
310			Sum=	$4,760

Figure A-3: Spreadsheet Section for Revised Calculation of Annual Damages

	A	B	C	D	E
294		Recurrence	Annual No.	Damages	Damages
295		Interval	of Events	and	And Losses
296		(Years)		Losses	
297		=+IF(ISNUMBER(B99),B99,"")	=IF(ISNUMBER(B297),1/B297,0)	=+H99	=IF(D297=0,0,EXP(0.5*(LN(D297)+LN(D298)))*(C297-C298))
298		=+IF(ISNUMBER(B100),B100,"")	=IF(ISNUMBER(B298),1/B298,0)	=+H100	=IF(D298=0,0,EXP(0.5*(LN(D298)+LN(D299)))*(C298-C299))
299		=+IF(ISNUMBER(B101),B101,"")	=IF(ISNUMBER(B299),1/B299,0)	=+H101	=IF(D299=0,0,EXP(0.5*(LN(D299)+LN(D300)))*(C299-C300))
300		=+IF(ISNUMBER(B102),B102,"")	=IF(ISNUMBER(B300),1/B300,0)	=+H102	=IF(D300=0,0,EXP(0.5*(LN(D300)+LN(D301)))*(C300-C301))
301		=+IF(ISNUMBER(B103),B103,"")	=IF(ISNUMBER(B301),1/B301,0)	=+H103	=IF(D301=0,0,EXP(0.5*(LN(D301)+LN(D302)))*(C301-C302))
302		=+IF(ISNUMBER(B104),B104,"")	=IF(ISNUMBER(B302),1/B302,0)	=+H104	=IF(D302=0,0,EXP(0.5*(LN(D302)+LN(D303)))*(C302-C303))
303		=+IF(ISNUMBER(B105),B105,"")	=IF(ISNUMBER(B303),1/B303,0)	=+H105	=IF(D303=0,0,EXP(0.5*(LN(D303)+LN(D304)))*(C303-C304))
304		=+IF(ISNUMBER(B106),B106,"")	=IF(ISNUMBER(B304),1/B304,0)	=+H106	=IF(D304=0,0,EXP(0.5*(LN(D304)+LN(D305)))*(C304-C305))
305		=+IF(ISNUMBER(B107),B107,"")	=IF(ISNUMBER(B305),1/B305,0)	=+H107	=IF(D305=0,0,EXP(0.5*(LN(D305)+LN(D306)))*(C305-C306))
306		=+IF(ISNUMBER(B108),B108,"")	=IF(ISNUMBER(B306),1/B306,0)	=+H108	=IF(D306=0,0,EXP(0.5*(LN(D306)+LN(D307)))*(C306-C307))
307		=+IF(ISNUMBER(B109),B109,"")	=IF(ISNUMBER(B307),1/B307,0)	=+H109	=IF(D307=0,0,EXP(0.5*(LN(D307)+LN(D308)))*(C307-C308))
308		=+IF(ISNUMBER(B110),B110,"")	=IF(ISNUMBER(B308),1/B308,0)	=+H110	=IF(D308=0,0,EXP(0.5*(LN(D308)+LN(D309)))*(C308-C309))
309		9999999	=IF(ISNUMBER(B309),1/B309,0)	=+D308	
310				Sum=	=+SUM(E297:E308)

Figure A-4: Spreadsheet Formulas for Revised Calculation of Annual Damages

Formulas in Figure A-4 show that the flood RIs are read from the input section into Column B and the Total Damages are read into Column D. Through calculations in a previous section of the spreadsheet the total damages for rows with no data are already set to the value in the previous row. The equation in Column C converts the RI value into Expected Annual Number of Occurrences (EANO) by taking the reciprocal of the RI. If RI for that row is a not given, EANO is set to zero.

The calculation of each band of the annualized damages is carried out in Column E. If the total damages for any row is zero, the annualized damage between that row and the next RI is set to zero. This ensures that benefits do not start until a RI with an actual damage value is reached. The annual damage of each band is calculated by taking the natural logarithm average of two sequential damages (evaluated by **EXP(0.5*(LN(D297)+LN(D298)))**) and multiplying the resulting value by the difference between the EANO values of the two levels **(C297-C298)**. For rows with no input data, the annualized damages would be zero. This formulation ensures that if the user chooses to input a larger RI with repeating total annual damage values (this would not happen under automatic interface to damage-frequency calculator), the sum of the annualized damages would remain unchanged. The revised spreadsheet allows up to 12 rows of input and calculations.

To ensure that the benefits from all events larger than the largest RI entered in the data are accounted for, an arbitrarily large number (9999999) is used as an additional RI to capture the benefits from the last frequency band.

The total of annual benefits is calculated in Cell E310 by summing the annual benefits from all rows in column E.

The calculation method described above, as well as other changes discussed in the report (e.g., number of calculation rows, label corrections, etc.) were implemented in the LD Module spreadsheet to generate a revised LD Module used in BCAR software development.